TRANSGENDER LIFE™

COMING OUT AS TRANSGENDER

CORONA BREZINA

ROSEN
PUBLISHING®

New York

Published in 2017 by The Rosen Publishing Group, Inc.
29 East 21st Street, New York, NY 10010

Library of Congress Cataloging-in-Publication Data

Names: Brezina, Corona, author.
Title: Coming out as transgender / Corona Brezina.
Description: First edition. | New York : Rosen Publishing, 2017. | Series: Transgender life | Includes bibliographical references and index.
Identifiers: LCCN 2016023152 | ISBN 9781508171812 (library bound) | ISBN 9781508171799 (pbk.) | ISBN 9781508171805 (6-pack)
Subjects: LCSH: Transgender people—Identity—Juvenile literature. | Transgenderism—Juvenile literature. | Coming out (Sexual orientation)—Juvenile literature.
Classification: LCC HQ77.9 .B746 2017 | DDC 306.76/8—dc23
LC record available at https://lccn.loc.gov/2016023152

Manufactured in China

Some of the images in this book illustrate individuals who are models. The depictions do not imply actual situations or events.

CONTENTS

INTRODUCTION

Coming out as transgender—the process of revealing your gender identity to family, friends, or the public—can be a daunting prospect. You should be prepared for shock or denial. You should also be ready to answer questions, such as "What does transgender mean?" and "What's gender identity?"

A *transgender* person is someone who identifies as a gender other than the one they were assigned at birth. A person's gender can be male, female, or some category other than those two. Gender identity is the gender that matches an individual's inner sense of gender. For trans people, their gender identities don't match their physical body or the gender role expected by society. *Gender expression* is the way in which a person chooses to show their gender identity.

Trans people only make up a small portion of the population—the book *Trans Bodies, Trans Selves* estimates that about .3 percent of the people in the United States are transgender. The opposite of transgender is *cisgender,* which describes people whose gender identities match their birth-assigned genders. Being cisgender is so prevalent that most people have never heard of the concept.

Coming out can be difficult because of possible reactions from family and friends, but it can also be scary because of the special challenges faced by transgender people. Unfortunately, trans people face the possibility of discrimination, harassment,

Louis Davies (*left*) and Jamie Eagle are a happy couple who are engaged to be married. Both are transgender and transitioning—Louis to male and Jamie to female.

misconceptions, and unwanted attention in many areas of life, from school to the workplace to medical care. Transgender youth are more likely than their peers to experience homelessness or to drop out of school.

If you prepare ahead of time before you come out, you may be able to help your family and friends better accept the news. Some parents and friends will be shaken but unsurprised, while others will find your disclosure utterly impossible to believe. You'll be ready to reassure them that you're still the same person they've always known and provide information about what it means to be transgender.

Throughout the process, you can benefit from the support of the trans community. Many large cities have trans organizations through which you can meet trans mentors and peers. Your school or community may have a LGBT (lesbian, gay, bisexual, and transgender) group you can join. The Internet can also provide invaluable resources for information and connect you to other trans people. In *Trans Bodies, Trans Selves*, transgender writer and activist Jennifer Finney Boylan praises the trans community:

> [It's] a community that is filled with breathtaking courage and compassion. The fact that many trans people are among the most disenfranchised and at-risk individuals in the world also means that we are frequently called upon to watch each other's backs, to exhibit a kind of loyalty and solidarity and courage that can only leave one stunned and amazed at the resilience of the human spirit.

It is important to remember that, while coming out can be a very difficult experience, you are not alone. Reach out to people in your life who will continue to support you, no matter how you express your gender identity, and remember to seek out the advice and support of those who have come out before you.

CHAPTER 1

COMING OUT TO YOURSELF

"**I**s the baby a boy or a girl?"

Your life may have begun with the doctor or nurse answering that question for your parents and telling them your birth-assigned gender. On the other hand, some parents learn their child's gender before the birth. They may have bought gender-specific clothing and toys months in advance of their new baby's arrival—pink for girls, blue for boys. These gender-specific items have little to do with biological sex and are instead dictated by societal expectations.

The terms "sex" and "gender" are not synonymous. An individual's *sex* is determined by anatomy and other biological characteristics, such as hormones and chromosomes. A person's *gender*, by contrast, is a social construction. Society expects men and women to fulfill certain expectations in terms of their behavior and activities. For example, in the United States, women are expected to devote more time to rearing children than men.

Pressure to conform to gender roles begins at an early age. Growing up, many transgender children reject clothes and toys intended for their birth-assigned gender.

Men are more likely than women to work in jobs requiring manual labor. Subtle expectations enter into everyday interactions, as well. Boys are generally expected to act more macho—talking about feelings or crying isn't considered a "guy thing." Girls, on the other hand, get the message that they're supposed to act more submissive; oftentimes, girls who assert themselves risk being called "bossy."

Many people chafe against restrictive notions of gender rules. Trans people, however, go further by questioning their very gender identity.

EXPERIENCING GENDER DYSPHORIA

For many trans people, exploration of their gender identity begins with *gender dysphoria*—the feeling of discomfort or anxiety about their birth-assigned gender. They feel that their body doesn't match their innate sense of being male, female, both, or neither. But articulating one's gender identity can be difficult, especially when one's society does not recognize genders other than male and female.

According to *Trans Bodies, Trans Selves,* "transgender" is,

> An umbrella term that may be used to describe people whose gender expression does not conform to cultural norms and/or whose gender identity is different from their sex assigned at birth. Transgender is a self-identity, and some gender nonconforming people do not identify with this term.

"Transgender," therefore, is not a narrowly defined third gender that can be placed alongside "male" and "female." It's a broad term that describes a range of gender identities.

Gender expression is the outward expression of gender identity. People express their gender through choices such as clothing, haircuts, and actions. Many trans people identify as a member of the gender opposite their birth-assigned gender. A female-to-male trans person, also called FTM or F2M, is someone who was assigned female at birth but identifies as a male—a trans man. Likewise, a male-to-female (MTF or M2F) was assigned male at birth but identifies as a trans woman. Trans people who identify as the opposite gender are sometimes called transsexual, and the term may refer specifically to a trans person who has had gender–affirming surgery. Transsexual is a narrower category than transgender—all transsexuals are transgender, but not all transgender people are transsexual. The broader term "transgender" is more commonly used today than "transsexual."

Other trans people identify themselves as neither male nor female. Gender can be viewed as a spectrum between male and female. Some people place their gender somewhere on the

KNOW YOUR PRONOUNS

For many transgender people, pronouns are an important milestone in their journey toward their affirmed gender—the gender reached during their transition. A trans man might ask to be referred to as "he" and "him" and a trans woman as "she" and "her." Some transgender people prefer gender-neutral pronouns, such as "they" and "them" used in a singular form, or the newer terms "ze" and "hir."

Pronouns are more significant than mere parts of speech to trans people. When others use the new pronouns naturally, it can convey acceptance of a trans person's gender identity. Alternately, failure to use preferred pronouns can be either a simple mistake or a sign of hostility. If someone messes up in using your pronouns, correct them calmly but firmly, and tell them that it's hurtful when they "mispronoun" you. Losing your temper won't help resolve the matter.

spectrum or completely reject traditional gender categories. They may label themselves gender variant, genderqueer, gender fluid, pangender, intergender, trigender, polygender, multigender, or all-gender. Trans people who identify with both male and female traits may call themselves androgynous or bigender. Those who reject gender designations may describe themselves as genderless, nongendered, gender-free, or agender. On the other side of the spectrum, some trans people reject highly specific labels. These trans men and trans women identify simply as men and women.

Many people make the mistake of thinking that all trans people are gay or lesbian. The misconception is easy to understand, since trans people are included under the LGBT umbrella, which is often used in discussing civil rights issues. Gender identity is unrelated to sexual orientation, which deals with people's sexual preferences. Like cisgender people, trans people can be gay, straight, bisexual, or some other category.

Likewise, cross-dressing—wearing the clothing of the opposite gender—is not an indicator that someone is transgender. (The older term, "transvestite," is considered offensive today.) Most cross-dressers are heterosexual men who enjoy wearing women's clothes but do not consider themselves female or wish to become female. Some gay men dress in drag on occasion, flamboyantly displaying themselves in women's clothing and accessories. Most drag queens dress up for self-expression and performance value, not to convey gender identity. Trans women dressing in women's clothing generally do not consider themselves to be cross-dressing or wearing drag, as their clothing is not donned as part of a performance but to express their gender identity.

A young man applies dramatic makeup as part of the elaborate preparation involved in dressing in drag. Dressing in drag represents a means of self-expression, not gender identity.

SELF-DISCOVERY AND SELF-ACCEPTANCE

Gender is a crucial concept to many trans people, and it's very important to them that a term exists that precisely describes their gender identity and expression. The array of terms and concepts might seem daunting to someone just learning about what it means to be transgender. If you're questioning your gender identity, you don't have to go down the list to choose the label you prefer. But once you do settle the matter, chances are that there's a word to describe your inclination.

Often, trans people begin questioning their gender identity when they realize that there's a mismatch between their bodies and their sense of self. The feeling is partly instinctive. When asked how they know they're transgender, many trans people say that they just *know*. More specifically, they may feel an aversion for the body parts and sexual characteristics of their birth-assigned gender. They might prefer activities and lifestyle habits typically associated with the "opposite" gender. They may feel that they don't relate to peers as their birth-assigned gender.

Trans people experiencing gender dysphoria may be surprised to learn that it's an official medical term, as it can cause significant psychological distress. Some trans people consider it offensive to have an aspect of their gender identity reduced to a medical diagnosis. Others point out that the diagnosis can facilitate access to medical care, such as counseling and treatments necessary for a physical transition.

Individuals can begin to question their gender identity at any age. Some trans people know from early childhood that they don't identify with their birth-assigned gender, while others come to consider themselves transgender later in life. It is important to know that when a person decides to transition does not make their experience or identity any less "authentic."

COMING OUT AS TRANSGENDER

Many trans people begin questioning their gender identity during adolescence. This can be a trying time of life for any teen, but it's often harder for transgender youth. They may be starting to experiment with a new identity at a time when most teenagers want to fit in with their peers. Transgender teens often experience self-doubt, wondering if there's something wrong with them or they're not normal. Puberty can be an especially difficult experience for them, as their bodies begin to change in respects that may be unwelcome.

If you're questioning your gender identity, you may need to come out to yourself first by acknowledging and exploring

For many teens, adolescence is a period for establishing independence and individuality. Transgender teens may explore their gender identity, as well.

your trans identity before you come out publicly. Learn about the different kinds of gender identity and try out different kinds of gender expression. Work to achieve some self-understanding before you try to explain it to the people around you.

Nevertheless, remember that making the transition to a new gender identity is a journey and that you can change course during the process. Someone might begin a transition from a woman to a man, for example, only to discover that they actually consider themselves somewhere else on the gender spectrum. It's also a lengthy process that involves social, medical, and legal aspects. Many young trans people are in a hurry to complete the transition to their authentic gender identity, but experts warn against rushing into the new role too quickly because of the psychological distress that can occur.

KEEPING YOUR BALANCE

Transgender people have a higher risk for suicide, depression, substance use, self-harm, and risky sexual behaviors than the general population. A 2010 survey conducted by the National Center for Transgender Equality and the National LGBTQ Task Force found that 41 percent of trans people had attempted suicide.

Trans people have a lot of issues to deal with related to their gender identity. Some live for years feeling out of place in their own body before they begin questioning their gender identity. The process of exploring gender identity and transitioning can be overwhelming. On top of that, trans people face stigma and hostility from society. Trans people experience discrimination in many aspects of their daily lives, and trans youth may be subjected to bullying or rejection by their peers. Some trans people are stressed when friends and family have trouble accepting their new gender status. This victimization and even violence can cause mental health issues for many trans people.

Take care of your mental health as you come to terms with your gender identity. Consider seeing a trans-friendly therapist even if you're not experiencing any mental health issues—a specialized mental health professional may be able to help you sort through issues during the process of questioning and transitioning. Also, learn about safe sex practices relevant to your gender identity. Trans people may experience challenges during transitioning and beyond, but many overcome these difficulties and become well-adjusted and happy in life.

CHAPTER 2

MAKING A PLAN

There's no single way to come out that will work best for every transgender individual. Trans teens have many factors to consider in deciding to disclose their gender identity, including both personal comfort and safety. It's natural that you don't want to hide an essential aspect of yourself from family and friends, but don't rush into the process. It will go more smoothly if you put thought into the circumstances beforehand.

Coming out trans is similar in some ways to coming out as gay, lesbian, or bisexual. Both take place after a period of questioning one's identity and achieving self-acceptance. Parents and friends may be astonished, or they may have suspected for a while. For gays, lesbians, and bisexuals, however, coming out is often the culmination of their self-realization. For trans people, it's a significant point on a journey toward their chosen gender identity. A trans person will probably have to explain what it means to be transgender when coming out. They will also have to describe what the future might hold, such as their plans to transition socially or medically to a different gender. A trans person may even have practice coming out—they initially may come out as gay, lesbian, or bisexual, then later come out as trans.

The support of friends, family, and organizations can help LGBT youth feel empowered rather than overwhelmed when struggling with sexual orientation and gender identity.

Unlike gays, lesbians, and bisexuals, who have the option of keeping their sexual orientation private, trans people may not have a choice about whether to share their gender identity with others. If a transgender person chooses to transition, their gender expression may reveal their gender identity. Some trans people say that their coming out is an ongoing process, as they continue to progress through different stages of their transition or understanding of their gender identity, and as they explain their gender identity to the people around them.

KNOW YOUR RIGHTS

Although transgender people are often subject to discrimination and harassment, there are legal recourses in some situations. The law varies drastically between states and even cities. Anti-discrimination laws prohibit discrimination in areas such as employment, housing, and public accommodations. Laws in some states protect transgender students in public schools from harassment and discrimination. Some federal laws protect transgender people by extending regulations banning discrimination based on sex to gender identity as well, and transgender people are included under the federal hate crimes law. Still, there is much progress to be made, especially in areas such as access to quality healthcare, employment and poverty issues, housing discrimination, and hate crimes. Laws concerning which bathroom transgender people use tend to be particularly controversial.

SETTING EXPECTATIONS

Coming out is a life-changing event. Most transgender people have a coming-out story, the circumstances under which they revealed their gender identity and the people they first told. For many, it's a huge relief to have their gender identity out in the

Some transgender kids are lucky enough to have parents who are accepting and fully supportive of their child's gender identity throughout the process of coming out and transitioning.

open. But family and friends can react badly, causing pain and strife for everyone involved.

Before deciding to come out to family and friends, consider both the benefits and potential difficulties of coming out. The benefits of coming out include the freedom of being open about your gender identity. You no longer have a secret weighing on your mind, and you may be relieved to share your authentic self with your family and friends. For those experiencing gender dysphoria, coming out may provide some alleviation of their emotional distress. It can also give trans teens an opportunity to support LGBT peers and take pride in LGBT issues.

The drawbacks to coming out mostly involve people's reactions. Friends might reject you, thinking that they never really knew you. Relationships are changed. You could face discrimination, ostracism, misunderstandings, and threats to your safety because of your gender identity. In addition, deciding to come out is a permanent decision. Once you've told people, you can't take it back.

You may feel instinctively that it's wrong to be living a lie, but for some people, revealing that they're transgender could endanger their health and safety. It's important to feel that you have a support system in place beforehand. If you believe that there could be significant negative consequences, you might consider waiting until you are free to make your own life choices and are not financially dependent on your parents. As a compromise, you could limit your coming out to telling a few trusted friends and family members.

Be prepared for both positive and negative reactions. Many people are relieved when their parents and friends react more supportively than they expected. Even when others do react badly, they often come to acceptance in time. Many trans people do report losing friends and alienating family members, however, so you should keep in mind that it could be a cost of your coming out.

Before making the decision to come out, confirm in your own mind that you're doing it for the right reasons. Questioning one's gender identity is a process that shouldn't be rushed. You should be comfortable in your own skin before you have to explain your gender identity to others. You shouldn't come out because of pressure from friends, to provoke a reaction, or to draw attention to yourself.

Try testing out reactions ahead of time. Casually bring up the topic of transgender issues to your parents, for example, or start a discussion about a transgender celebrity with your friends to learn their opinions. In this way, you can gauge whether you're likely to have a supportive home environment and safe conditions at school.

WHO DO YOU TELL?

You also have to decide who you're going to come out to and plan your strategy. Are you planning to tell just the people close to you, or are you going to come out publicly? If you only want to tell a few people, you should probably emphasize to them that you're still keeping your gender identity private. Remind them not to discuss the topic on social media, where it might inadvertently be shared widely. Also remember that it could be uncomfortable if you ask people to keep your gender identity a secret from people they're close to—for example, telling one sibling but not another, or telling just one person out of a close group of friends.

Many people start out by telling a close friend whom they believe will be supportive. Choose someone you know will take

Revealing your gender identity can make friendships feel more honest and authentic, but be prepared for your news to change the nature of some relationships.

your statement of your gender identity seriously, someone who tends to keep a level head in unforeseen circumstances. It will boost your confidence if the first person you tell reacts well to the news. You'll also feel better knowing that you have an ally as you prepare to come out to people who may be more resistant to the idea.

When trans adults come out, old friends can be bewildered and even betrayed that someone they knew suddenly seems transformed into a different person. Your teenage friends might be more open to the idea of shaping and experimenting with aspects of identity, even gender identity. Nonetheless, changing your gender means that the way you socialize with your peers may change. If you have a girlfriend or boyfriend, in particular, your coming out could raise issues of compatibility. Be prepared for the possible end of the relationship, since your partner would essentially have to adjust his or her sexual orientation in order to stay with you.

Trans people often find that the hardest part of coming out is telling their parents. Most kids long for their parents' approval,

Living openly as transgender can be problematic in some work environments. Math teacher Christian Zsilavetz was told not to reveal his transgender identity to his students.

even if the relationship is sometimes difficult. The prospect that parents might reject their trans son or daughter can feel heartbreaking. It can be a huge shock for parents and require a substantial adjustment. They may feel like they're losing a son or daughter. On the other hand, you may find that your parents already had some notion that you were different. If you have reason to believe that your safety and health would be at risk when you tell your parents, though, you may want to consider waiting to come out to them until you're more independent.

Coming out can be a gradual process as you come out to more people and, perhaps, publicly at school, at work, and to your extended circle of family and friends. Before you make that decision, talk to adults you trust, such as a guidance counselor, teacher, or boss. Make sure that you have a support system and that you'll be safe in your school and work environment. Be prepared for the possibility of discrimination and misunderstandings, even if you're pretty certain you'll be comfortable being openly transgender at school. Many trans youth do thrive in school, especially in schools that have sound policies for supporting trans students.

CHAPTER 3

COMING OUT TO FAMILY AND FRIENDS

You probably don't want to come out to your family and friends by saying, "Guess what? I'm transgender!" But even if you are nervous and perhaps dreading the encounter, you should focus on the positive aspects of the news. You're acting on a decision that you believe will make you happier and more fulfilled in your own life. It's important to demonstrate confidence when you first tell people close to you that you're transgender. You're disclosing a part of your identity, not hosting a debate over whether you're really transgender.

Be prepared for a barrage of questions about your news. Beforehand, do some research so that you can have answers ready. Learning about transgender issues will help you learn more about your gender identity as well as prepare you for coming out. You should be able to share information about what it means to be transgender, as well as an explanation of your personal gender

The parents of North Carolina teen Hunter Schafer initially resisted the idea that their child was transgender, but they came to accept that she did not identify as male.

identity. Try rehearsing your response to possible reactions ahead of time. Some experts suggest preparing for the worst reaction but not necessarily assuming that you'll get a negative reaction.

You should also provide your family and friends with information about transgender people and transgender issues. The organization PFLAG (formerly known as Parents, Family and Friends of Lesbians and Gays) provides resources, information, and services. Many LGBT centers also have support groups for the family and friends of transgender people.

YOUR SUPPORT SYSTEMS

During your transition, you will benefit from the expertise of trans-friendly counselors, therapists, doctors, and other medical professionals. Make an effort to find general practitioners and mental health workers who are experienced in treating transgender teens. Trans organizations and the internet can help you find health providers familiar with transgender medical practices.

Many young people start with a visit to a gender clinic that specializes in treating transgender children and young adults. Transgender adolescents are usually treated by a pediatric endocrinologist—a doctor specializing in hormone issues that affect growth and sexual development. Pediatric endocrinologists can help chart a path to medical transition for transgender teens, while mental health workers can address issues regarding gender dysphoria. Some gender clinics also provide advocacy and legal support.

HAVING THE CONVERSATION

When you're ready to come out to your family or friends, choose an appropriate place and time. Avoid coming out to your family during high-stress situations such as the holidays, for example.

Pick a safe, neutral setting where you can have adequate privacy and plenty of time to talk.

Consider writing a letter telling people about your gender identity. Some trans people choose to come out through a letter or online communication. If you decide to tell your family and friends in person instead—and this is probably the better course of action when dealing with those closest to you—composing a letter will help you get your thoughts together. You might want to give them a letter after you have the conversation to reassure them that everything will be OK and tell them how much you would appreciate their support.

Set a tone for the talk—be confident, calm, and straightforward. Confidence can be crucial in persuading others that you're certain about your gender identity. Don't argue or allow the situation to become confrontational. Try to reassure them that acknowledging your authentic gender identity doesn't mean that you're turning into another person.

Keep it simple, and don't give them too much information at first. Your initial disclosure isn't the time to

Writing a letter describing your sense of gender identity can help you clarify your own thoughts, as well as inform others that you're transgender.

go into details about your plans for transitioning. Avoid using specific terminology that they won't understand. Don't tell them immediately that you're going to change your name. Instead, talk about your personal experiences and difficulties. Describe the emotional pain you've been feeling and the struggle to understand the root cause. You're coming out to people because you believe that it will make things better for you over the long term, and you're asking for their support.

When talking to your parents or others very close to you, be prepared for extreme emotions during the disclosure. You might already anticipate the possible emotional reactions—anger or shock on one side, affirmation of love on the other. But there's no way you can anticipate the sheer force of the response. You'll be wracked with your emotions, as well, from near terror over coming out to relief at their acceptance or the pain of rejection.

HAVE PATIENCE

Some families recognize and accept their child as transgender from an early age; others disown a son or daughter who comes out as trans. Most reactions will fall in between these extremes. People will need time to get used to the idea, and the conversation will continue as your friends and family come to terms with your gender identity.

The news will probably catch your family and friends off guard. Initial reactions may be more extreme than long-term responses. Once they have a chance to think it over, people often become more accepting. Be prepared to see some friends drift away, however, even if they seem to handle your coming out well.

Parents often feel a sense of guilt when their son or daughter comes out. They may wonder if it was their fault that there's

Coy Mathis' birth-assigned gender is male, but from a young age, she wanted to live as a girl. Coy's family and friends came to accept her as a girl.

something "wrong" with you because of how they raised you. Others feel guilty because their child was experiencing inner pain and they failed to notice or act.

The people closest to you may have reactions similar to those who are grieving: denial, anger, bargaining, depression, and, finally, acceptance. Parents, in particular, may feel a sense of loss. From your early years, they held certain expectations of you based on your gender. Even if they embrace your new gender identity, they'll have to replace some of their old dreams for your future with new scenarios. Reassure them that although you're revealing a new aspect of who you are, you're still the same person they've always known.

Recognize that many reactions you view as negative may really be rooted in concern for your well-being. Trans people face many obstacles that cisgender people don't have to consider. Your family and friends may be worried about your safety, health, and future. They don't want to see you rejected by others because of your gender identity.

Unlike the coming out of gays, lesbians, and bisexuals coming out as transgender is a long-term process. You may begin a social and physical transition, which will be accompanied by a deepening understanding of your own gender identity. Even if your family and friends are supportive of your coming out, the various aspects of your transition might cause aftershocks. They might have no trouble accepting the idea of your gender expression, for example, but they could need time to get used to seeing you wearing clothes associated with the opposite gender.

BEING OUTED

One danger of keeping your gender identity private is the possibility of being publicly outed against your wishes. Being outed means that someone disclosed that you're transgender without your permission or approval. Maybe you told a friend who failed to keep it confidential. Maybe you left an information trail or an open browser on your computer when you were researching trans issues—a surprising number of people get discovered in this way. Maybe someone at your school just guessed, and you confirmed it with your reaction.

Being outed can occur at various points in your journey. For example, perhaps you've decided that you're going to keep your gender identity private and wait to live openly until you've graduated high school. You might want to avoid facing tons of questions and potential discrimination in your school. Being outed forces you to explain and defend yourself in public perhaps before you've fully come to terms with your gender identity.

Alternately, being outed could mean revealing that a person's expressed gender doesn't match their birth gender. If a trans person chooses to fully transition to their authentic gender identity and live as a woman or man without acknowledging their birth gender, the consequences of being outed can be devastating. It can shatter their emotional well-being and impact their personal and professional lives. Trans people have committed suicide or had their careers ruined as a result of being outed.

If you have been outed, you probably feel betrayed and caught off guard, whether it's a friend telling a mutual friend or a classmate telling the entire cafeteria. Nonetheless, you're forced to react with no chance to prepare, when you would have preferred to initiate any discussion of your gender identity yourself. Assess the situation and decide how to respond. You could explain on the spot or else say that you're not ready to discuss the subject. Don't feel obligated to share more than you're comfortable disclosing. If you feel that your safety is in jeopardy, get help from a friend, school official, or other authority.

Transgender issues can arouse strong feelings of hostility or support. Here, students inaugurate a new gender-neutral bathroom in their school.

After the fact, enlist support from your friends or school officials. Check if your school has a policy for supporting transgender students. Emphasize that outing a trans person is a violation of trust and a potential catalyst for discrimination and other unwanted attention.

CHAPTER 4

DEALING WITH REACTIONS

The reactions from your family and friends when you come out as transgender can range from utter rejection to full support. You may observe some initial awkwardness as people get used to the idea of your gender identity. They're being asked to make a major shift in how they think of you, and hopefully most will manage it. The nature of some of your friendships may change, but that's inevitable as young people mature and look toward the future, even when being transgender isn't a factor.

As you become accustomed to living openly, whether you're out publicly or just to a few friends, you'll find that people react with a range of attitudes toward transgender people. Some of your friends may be trans allies who support transgender rights, while others may accept you but express little interest in trans issues. On the negative side, you'll encounter outright hostility from some people and microaggressions from others. Microaggresions are verbal or nonverbal slights or snubs that subtly disparage members of marginalized groups. Examples

Many transgender people begin dressing in clothes typically associated with their true gender and experimenting with new hairstyles during their social transition.

might include the implication that a trans man or trans woman isn't a "real" man or woman, or a so-called friend's failure to make an effort to use a trans person's correct pronouns. You'll come to appreciate your true friends even more and learn to deal with intolerance and misunderstandings from others.

SO MANY QUESTIONS

As mentioned previously, reactions to your coming out will vary widely, from shock and doubt to guilt and confusion. Their responses will reflect this wide range. People will ask you basic factual questions about being transgender. You should also expect to be asked about your personal sense of gender identity. Some responses will be more about the person reacting to your news than about you. Here are a few examples of common questions and comments:

- "How do you know?" Instead of saying "I just know," give them some specific examples about how you've struggled and come to terms with your gender identity.
- "I'll never be able to see you as a woman/man" or "I can't handle this." Say that plenty of family and friends of transgender people have come to terms with the notion of being transgender. Steer them to resources for trans allies. Instead of getting angry, assure them that you're there to talk about it if they need to and that you hope that they'll come to change their minds.
- From parents: "What did we do to cause this?" Tell them that it's not fully known what makes someone transgender, but experts believe that factors such as genes, hormones, and life experiences all contribute. Parents' childrearing practices do not cause a child to become transgender.
- "It's just a phase." Explain that transgender people often realize from a young age that there's a mismatch between their birth-assigned gender and their gender identity. It's normal for any kid to experiment with aspects of gender, but trans people are consistent over time in their gender identity.
- "But what about getting married and having kids?" Tell them that it's still entirely possible for you to marry and have children. Trans people have many of the same options open to any other single or childless adult.
- "Are you going to take hormones?" or "Does this mean you're going to have surgery?" You're still allowed privacy as you're

coming out and making a transition. Don't hesitate to decline to answer explicit questions about your body or your plans about dating, for example. Tell them that you're not comfortable answering such personal questions or discussing medical information. After all, would they ask a cisgender person such intrusive questions?

- "But you're biologically male (or female)" or "Are you going to have a sex change?" In addition to saying that you'd rather not answer invasive questions, you can explain to people that someone's gender identity doesn't *always* match their

If you're coming out as trans, you may find greatest acceptance among your peers—in general, younger Americans are more supportive of transgender rights.

birth-assigned gender. You can also mention that the term "sex change" is sometimes considered derogatory and the preferred term is "gender-affirmationing surgery."

- "What pronouns should I use to describe you?", "Do you want me to keep your gender identity private from others?" or "What can I do to support you?" These are a few questions you might receive from someone who is knowledgeable and sensitive about trans topics. Plenty of people are aware of trans issues and supportive of trans individuals, and you can help inform your family and friends.

BAD REACTIONS

Even if you hope that your family and friends will adjust to the disclosure of your gender identity, you should prepare for the eventuality that some people won't handle the news well. You may lose friends and even be rejected by family members.

Family and friends of trans people who react badly at first often get used to the idea, but sometimes they fail to become supporters. In some cases, the relationship might reach a stalemate. A friend or family member may continue to accept you as an individual but refuse to address the issue of your gender identity. Worse, people might actively condemn the fact of you being transgender. A parent, for example, might believe that being transgender is morally wrong, blame your shortcomings on your gender identity, or insist that being transgender is something you can change if you try hard enough.

The worst-case scenario for a trans youth is when parents cut off their transgender child. Being kicked out of the house is a real danger for trans teenagers. LGBT young people are disproportionately likely to become homeless, and once they're on the street, they are in greater danger of being sexually assaulted. Some get caught up in the juvenile justice system as a consequence of drug use and breaking the law just to survive.

If you think there's any danger that your parents could cast you out or turn to violence when you come out to them, plan ahead for that contingency. Arrange beforehand to stay with a friend if necessary. Have a bag packed with essential items in case you're forced to leave home quickly. Look up youth shelters that are LGTB friendly and find out if there are any organizations in your area that could help you. Make sure that

A candlelight vigil is held in remembrance of transgender individuals who died in India. Worldwide, transgender people are at a higher risk of discrimination and violence.

you have enough money to support yourself financially for the short-term. Even better, save up ahead of time in case you end up living on your own.

Trans teens sometimes end up running away from hostile home environments. Unless you feel that your health and safety are at risk, try to reach an understanding with your parents and remain at home even if they refuse to accept your gender identity. The alternatives—such as living on the streets and failing to complete high school—are much worse. It will get better for you once you're older and in charge of your own life. In the meantime, do your best to prepare for a bright future.

DEALING WITH BULLYING AND HARASSMENT

Sadly, most transgender youth experience bullying and harassment in school. According to a 2010 survey on transgender discrimination, 78 percent of trans respondents had been harassed at school, and 35 percent had been physically assaulted. Turning to school personnel wasn't necessarily a solution for bullied trans teens—31 percent had been harassed by teachers or staff.

Intolerance and discriminatory treatment toward trans people is sometimes called transphobia. If you've been bullied or harassed for being transgender, the first step is recognizing it. Bullying can be physical, verbal, or relational. Physical bullying is easy to recognize, but taunting, threats, ostracism, vicious rumors, and public shaming are also forms of bullying. Cyberbullying can also be devastating.

(continued on the next page)

(continued from the previous page)

Cyberbullies can attack their victims in their own home, at any time, sometimes anonymously.

Despite the dire statistics, trans students are more likely to be supported at school today than in the past. Public awareness of transgender people and trans issues has increased. Schools are more likely to have antibullying policies and plans in place to protect transgender students. If you're bullied for being transgender, tell your parents and report it to a teacher or other school personnel. If they don't take sufficient action to protect you, tell another adult authority figure. The government's official site to prevent bullying, StopBullying.gov, recommends, "Try talking to as many adults as possible if there's a problem—teachers, counselors, custodians, nurses, parents. The more adults they involve, the better."

NEGOTIATING CULTURAL NORMS

Coming out changes more than your relationships with the individuals closest to you. You're probably prepared for the reactions of family and friends, but what about the larger circle of people around you? Examples include your church or religious community, your cultural or ethnic group, or social groups related to extracurricular interests. Transgender people come from every racial and socioeconomic group. Each trans person has a unique journey ahead of them.

You'll have to negotiate how you fit into these different circles with your new gender identity. How do you respond to a religion that rejects your gender identity? What do you do when you

Destin Cramer (*second from right*) embraces friends from the Gender Awareness Group that he founded in his Seattle, Washington, high school.

have to sign up for a "men's" or "women's" sports team? How do you talk to your extended family when you're from a cultural background in which the language doesn't even have a word for "transgender"? How do you introduce and identify yourself when you're suddenly immersed in a new group of peers, such as when you go to summer camp? You might feel isolated if you suddenly find yourself to be something of an outsider in a community that has been important in your life. Nevertheless, you'll gradually acquire confidence and experience in deciding how to express your gender identity and when to disclose it, depending on safety and personal comfort.

CHAPTER 5

THE SOCIAL TRANSITION AND BEYOND

Once someone has come out as transgender, what's next? For most trans people, transforming their gender expression—or maybe just tweaking it—to match their gender identity is a journey, and coming out is just one step. The process is different for everyone depending on their sense of self. For many, there's some degree of experimentation or trial and error before they find the gender expression that fits them best.

Most trans people make a social transition, during which they take on aspects of their affirmed gender without undergoing medical intervention. Some, but not all, also undergo a medical transition, in which they may take hormones and undergo surgery that alters their bodies to match their affirmed gender. They may also take further measures to alter how they present themselves physically, such as permanent hair removal or voice training. Transgender teens may think about these issues as they

Activism by transgender celebrities such as actress Laverne Cox has helped raise public awareness and dispel misconceptions about trans people and transgender issues.

come out and try out new means of gender expression, but a medical transition is unlikely to be an immediate prospect for adolescents.

Some people want to use every possible means to correspond to their affirmed gender. Others are comfortable with a gender expression that involves both male and female aspects. After all, plenty of cisgender people have traits or interests that are typically associated with the opposite gender.

There's no reason that trans people should feel compelled to restrict their gender identity or expression to fit a narrow concept of "woman" or "man."

GENDER ROLES AND RULES

Many trans people talk of how they knew from a young age that they didn't correspond with their birth-assigned gender and rebelled against gender norms. Young boys demanded to wear pink shirts showing images of their favorite cartoon princesses. Young girls refused to wear dresses. During adolescence, when teens go through puberty, clothes and other signifiers of gender expression become more important. A teenage trans person

Even as they try to fit in with peers, today's young people respect and appreciate diversity of race, ethnicity, gender, religion, ideology, and gender identity in the people around them.

may be trying out the gender role that they plan to take on as an adult.

Some trans people making a social transition to their affirmed gender choose to accentuate certain traits associated with that gender. Trans women may experiment with makeup; trans men might bind their breasts. Trans people may begin to try out clothing of the opposite gender and encounter challenges in finding the ideal pieces. Trans men sometimes have difficulty in finding men's clothing in their sizes, and trans women sometimes require larger shoes than are widely available. Hairstyles also provide a means of self-expression and an opportunity for experimentation.

Trans people also have to navigate a new set of expectations in social settings. You might find that you relate differently with your friends of both genders through no fault of your own. Many trans people discover that people interact differently when they're with a group of friends of the same gender than when they're in a mixed gender group. Because of social expectations, "girl talk" and "guy talk" really are two different kinds of communication. Likewise, trans people who have fully transitioned to their affirmed gender report that people they encounter in their everyday lives treat them differently depending on their perceived gender.

Dating can be stressful for most teens, and being transgender adds another complication. Whether your partner is cisgender or trans, clear communication can prevent misunderstandings. If you're not openly out, you will have to disclose your transgender status at some point in the relationship. Many trans people choose to disclose this soon after becoming involved with a partner.

As you work your way through your social transition and gain confidence in your gender expression, don't neglect your schoolwork and interests, whether you're into sports or theater.

Personal and group activities will give you an opportunity to grow as a human being, spend time with the friends who supported you as you came out as transgender, and cultivate new friends, perhaps as an openly trans teen.

AN ONGOING JOURNEY

During adolescence, puberty begins to bring about drastic changes in teens' bodies. These include development of visible traits—girls develop breasts; boys acquire facial hair, Adam's apples, deeper voices, and more masculine facial structures. These are all features that transgender people may choose to have surgically altered later in life. Some transgender teens choose to delay the onset of puberty by taking hormones called

As a teen, Andii Viveros fought for transgender rights and was accepted as female by her parents and peers—she was even elected prom queen.

puberty blockers. The effect is reversible, and puberty resumes once the blockers are stopped. Delaying puberty gives trans teens an extended opportunity to explore their gender identity before physical changes occur.

WHAT'S IN A NAME?

Most trans people take new names when they come out. It can represent a new beginning or a transformation, and trans people sometimes refer to their original names as their "dead names." Many people choose a new name that's related to their original— Christopher to Christine, for example—but there's no single formula for choosing a new name. Sometimes people pick a common or gender-neutral name so that they won't stand out, while others choose a name that emphasizes their individuality. Trans people might opt for a name that is a tribute to someone they admire or one that reflects their ethnic origins. Some trans people say that they've identified themselves by a specific name privately for a long time.

Sometimes trans people choose to change their surnames as well as their first names. There are numerous reasons they might do so. For example, they may want to distance themselves from their old name out of concern for safety or privacy. Maybe they just want a fresh start or like the way their new name sounds. Regardless, legally changing both first and last names for any reason (other than fraud) is not a difficult process.

In most cases, parents have control over a teen's medical decisions. As you come out as transgender and begin to transition socially, do your best to keep your parents informed about how you're doing. Your medical dealings will proceed more smoothly if your parents are supportive and knowledgeable about transgender youth issues and options. Remember, there are possible risks, complications, and side effects to all medical interventions.

Many transgender people who wish to undergo a medical transition are in a hurry to complete the process so that they can live as their authentic selves. But a full physical transition takes a long time and requires many separate steps. Most doctors involved in the process follow guidelines known as the Standards of Care developed by the World Professional Association for Transgender Health. These guidelines direct medical professionals to accepted medical options that emphasize the well-being and self-fulfillment of transgender people during their transition.

Transgender people often begin their physical transition by seeing a gender therapist, usually for a period of three to six months, in order to be referred to a doctor for hormone treatments that will feminize or masculinize the body. Estrogen and other hormones cause breast development, redistribute fat around the body, and reduce hair growth in trans women. Testosterone treatments bring about deeper voices, greater muscle mass, and the cessation of menstruation in trans men. Some of the changes brought about by hormone treatments are reversible; others are permanent. Trans people must continue taking hormones for life.

If a trans person decides to undergo a surgical transition, they may be required to complete a year of real-life experience (RLE) beforehand, in which they live openly as their affirmed gender. Possible surgeries include top surgery that augments or removes the breasts and bottom surgery that involves genital

Many LGBT people and their allies go beyond mere acceptance of different sexual orientations and gender identities and publicly show pride in who they are.

reconstruction, facial surgery, and reduction of the Adam's apple. Trans people who have taken puberty blockers before the physical transition require fewer surgical interventions.

Trans people who have completed their transition—whatever the extent—may choose either to live openly as trans or live as their affirmed gender. This is sometimes referred to as "living stealth," "living privately," or "passing." For some trans people, living privately affirms their gender identity. They may also feel safer and more comfortable fitting in without having to come out to everyone they meet. Others are proud of their transgender status and do not feel a need to be seen as cisgender.

If you've attended the same high school your whole life, your peers will probably be aware that you are transgender. But if you transfer to a school where you're the new kid, you may have the option of either living openly or privately, depending on your school's policies.

Later in life, you may also have to deal with the legal aspects of being transgender. Some transgender people opt to change their legal name and gender on identification documents. Laws and procedures for changing name and gender on driver's licenses and birth certificates vary from state to state.

When you first come out, people may react by saying, "But things are going to be so difficult for you!" It's true that trans people face challenges that cisgender people never have. But trans people rarely regret their journey, which sometimes leads to insights into their own personal identity that cisgender people never have to consider. You can respond to such reactions by saying that everyone faces obstacles in life, and being able to achieve a gender expression that matches your own sense of self is worth the hardships.

GLOSSARY

AFFIRMED GENDER The gender that a transgender person transitions to.

ALLY A supporter; for example, a cisgender person who advocates for transgender people.

CISGENDER Describing someone whose gender identity matches their birth-assigned gender.

COMING OUT Revealing one's gender identity.

DISCLOSURE The act of sharing one's gender identity in a certain instance.

DISCRIMINATION Prejudicial treatment of members of a certain group, based on class, religion, race, gender, or sexual orientation.

GENDER DYSPHORIA A medical diagnosis describing a person's emotional distress over a mismatch between their birth-assigned gender and gender identity.

GENDER EXPRESSION Outward manifestations of gender, such as clothes, mannerisms, and social interactions, which are perceived as masculine or feminine.

GENDER IDENTITY A person's internal sense of being male, female, both, or neither.

HARASSMENT Any unwelcome conduct that is repeated and used to intimidate.

HORMONE A chemical messenger in the body that affects the functions of various tissues and organs.

LGBT An acronym signifying lesbian, gay, bisexual, and transgender.

MEDICAL TRANSITION The process of changing one's body through hormones or surgery to affirm gender identity. Related terms are "physical transition" and "surgical transition."

POLICY A course of action adopted by a school, government, business, or other group.

PRIVACY The right to be left alone from interference by the government or other people.

PUBERTY The stage of life in which an adolescent reaches sexual maturity and becomes capable of reproduction.

SOCIAL TRANSITION The process of affirming one's gender identity in daily life, such as through clothing, grooming, and pronouns.

TRANSGENDER Describing someone whose gender identity does not match their birth-assigned gender.

TRANSITION The process a transgender person undertakes to live as their affirmed gender.

TRANSSEXUAL A person whose gender identity does not match their birth-assigned gender; specifically, someone who has undergone a physical transition affirming gender.

FOR MORE INFORMATION

Egale Canada Human Rights Trust

185 Carlton Street

Toronto, ON M5A 2K7

Canada

(416) 964-7887

Website: http://egale.ca

Since 1995, Egale has actively worked to create a world without homophobia, biphobia, or transphobia through research, education, and community engagement.

Gender Spectrum

1271 Washington Avenue #834

San Leandro, CA 94577

(510) 788-4412

Email: info@genderspectrum.org

Website: https://www.genderspectrum.org

Gender Spectrum helps to create a gender sensitive and inclusive environment for children and teens by providing consultation services, training, and educational events.

National Center for Transgender Equality (NCTE)

1400 16th Street NW, Suite 510

Washington, DC 20036

(202) 642-4542

Email: ncte@transequality.org

Website: http://www.transequality.org

Founded in 2003 by transgender activists, the National Center for Transgender Equality works at the local, state, and federal level to advance transgender equality through laws, policies, and societal change.

PFLAG National Office
1828 L Street NW, Suite 660
Washington, DC 20036
(202) 467-8180
Fax: (202) 467-8194
Email: info@pflag.org
Website: http://www.pflag.org
Uniting people who are lesbian, gay, bisexual, transgender, and queer (LGBTQ) with families, friends, and allies, PFLAG is committed to advancing equality and full societal affirmation of LGBTQ people through its threefold mission of support, education, and advocacy.

Trans Equality Society of Alberta (TESA)
PO Box 2053
Edmonton, AB T5J 2P4
Canada
Website: http://www.tesaonline.org
TESA's mission is to be a voice for trans people in Alberta through advocacy and education in government and community service.

Transgender Law Center
1629 Telegraph Avenue, Suite 400
Oakland, CA 94612
(415) 865-0176
Fax: (877) 847-1278
Email: info@transgenderlawcenter.org
Website: http://transgenderlawcenter.org

The Transgender Law Center works to change law, policy, and attitudes so that all people, regardless of their gender identity or expression, can live safely and freely.

TransYouth Family Allies (TYFA)
PO Box 1471
Holland, MI 49422-1471
(888) 462-8932
Email: info@imatyfa.org
Website: http://www.imatyfa.org
TYFA was founded in 2006 and has helped thousands of families and their children since then through education, outreach, and support.

The Trevor Project
PO Box 69232
West Hollywood, CA 90069
(310) 271-8845
24/7 Hotline: (866) 488-7386
Website: http://www.thetrevorproject.org
The Trevor Project provides crisis intervention and suicide prevention services, most notably a twenty-four-hour hotline, to lesbian, gay, bisexual, transgender, and questioning youth.

WEBSITES

Because of the changing nature of internet links, Rosen Publishing has developed an online list of websites related to the subject of this book. This site is updated regularly. Please use this link to access the list:

http://www.rosenlinks.com/TL/out

FOR FURTHER READING

Andrews, Arin. *Some Assembly Required: The Not-So-Secret Life of a Transgender Teen.* New York, NY: Simon & Schuster Books for Young Readers, 2014.

Belge, Kathy, and Marke Bieschke. *Queer: The Ultimate LGBT Guide for Teens.* San Francisco, CA: Zest Books, 2011.

Bono, Chaz. *Transition: The Story of How I Became a Man.* New York, NY: Dutton, 2011.

Bornstein, Kate, and S. Bear Bergman. *Gender Outlaws: The Next Generation.* Berkeley, CA: Seal Press, 2010.

Boylan, Jennifer Finney. *She's Not There: A Life in Two Genders.* New York, NY: Broadway Books, 2013.

Brezenoff, Steve. *Brooklyn Burning.* Minneapolis, MN: Carolrhoda Books, 2014.

Gold, Rachel. *Being Emily.* Tallahassee, FL: Bella Books, 2012.

Killermann, Sam. *The Social Justice Advocate's Handbook: A Guide to Gender.* Austin, TX: Impetus Books, 2013.

Kuklin, Susan. *Beyond Magenta: Transgender Teens Speak Out.* Somerville, MA: Candlewick Press, 2015.

Nutt, Amy Ellis. *Becoming Nicole: The Transformation of an American Family.* New York, NY: Random House, 2015.

Petrow, Steve, and Sally Chew. *Steve Petrow's Complete Gay and Lesbian Manners: The Definitive Guide to LGBT Life.* New York, NY: Workman Publishing, 2011.

Savage, Dan, and Terry Miller, eds. *It Gets Better: Coming Out, Overcoming Bullying, and Creating a Life Worth Living.* New York, NY: Dutton, 2011.

Seba, Jaime A. *Feeling Wrong in Your Own Body: Understanding*

What It Means to Be Transgender. Broomall, PA: Mason Crest Publishers, 2011.

Spoon, Rae, and Ivan Coyote. *Gender Failure.* Vancouver, Canada: Arsenal Pulp, 2014.

Testa, Rylan Jay, et. al. *The Gender Quest Workbook: A Guide for Teens and Young Adults Exploring Gender Identity.* Oakland, CA: Instant Help Books, 2015.

Wittlinger, Ellen. *Parrotfish.* New York, NY: Simon & Schuster Books for Young Readers, 2015.

BIBLIOGRAPHY

"Answers to Your Questions About Transgender People, Gender Identity and Gender Expression." American Psychological Association, 2016 (http://www.apa.org/topics/lgbt/transgender.aspx).

Barz, Erica, and Liz Owen. "Our Trans Loved Ones: Questions and Answers for Parents, Families, and Friends of People Who Are Transgender and Gender Expansive." PFLAG, 2015 (http://community.pflag.org/document.doc?id=921).

Brill, Stephanie, and Rachel Pepper. *The Transgender Child: A Handbook for Families and Professionals.* San Francisco, CA: Cleis Press, 2008.

"Coming Out: A Coming Out Guide forTrans Young People." LGBT Youth Scotland, 2016 (http://www.teni.ie/attachments /664c0589-3011-46a5-a6a3-28269015b71b.PDF)

Erickson-Schroth, Laura, ed. *Trans Bodies, Trans Selves: A Resource for the Transgender Community.* New York, NY: Oxford University Press, 2014.

"Gay and Transgender Youth Homelessness by the Numbers." Center for American Progress, June 21, 2010 (https://www.americanprogress.org/issues/lgbt/news/2010/06/21/7980/gay-and-transgender-youth-homelessness-by-the-numbers/).

Glicksman, Eve. "Transgender Today." American Psychological Association, April 2013 (http://www.apa.org/monitor/2013/04/transgender.aspx).

Goo, Sara Kehaulani. "Among Transgender Adults, Stories About a 'Difficult' Transition." Pew Research Center, April 28, 2015 (http://www.pewresearch.org/fact-tank/2015/04/28/transgender-adults/).

Grant, Jaime M., et. al. "Injustice at Every Turn: A Report of the National Transgender Discrimination Survey." National Center for Transgender Equality and National LGBTQ Task Force, 2011 (http://www.thetaskforce.org/static_html/downloads/reports/reports/ntds_full.pdf).

"Guide to Being a Trans Ally." PFLAG, 2014 (http://community.pflag.org/document.doc?id=904).

Huegel, Kelly. *GLBTQ: The Survival Guide for Gay, Lesbian, Bisexual, Transgender, and Questioning Teens.* Minneapolis, MN: Free Spirit Publishing, 2011.

Lopez, German. "9 Questions About Gender Identity and Being Transgender You Were Too Embarrassed to Ask." *Vox*, September 21, 2015 (http://www.vox.com/2015/4/24/8483561/transgender-gender-identity-expression).

Moskowitz, Clara. "High Suicide Risk, Prejudice Plague Transgender People. *LiveScience,* November 19, 2010 (http://www.livescience.com/11208-high-suicide-risk-prejudice-plague-transgender-people.html).

Orr, Asaf, et. al. "Schools in Transition: A Guide for Supporting Transgender Students in K-12 Schools." ACLU et al., 2015 (http://www.nclrights.org/wp-content/uploads/2015/08/Schools-in-Transition-2015.pdf).

Pepper, Rachel, ed. *Transitions of the Heart: Stories of Love, Struggle and Acceptance by Mothers of Transgender and Gender Variant Children.* San Francisco, CA: Cleis Press, 2012.

StopBullying.gov. US Department of Health & Human Services, 2016 (http://www.stopbullying.gov/).

Teich, Nicholas M. *Transgender 101.* New York, NY: Columbia University Press, 2012.

"Trans and Gender Nonconforming Identities." Planned Parenthood, 2014 (https://www.plannedparenthood.org/learn/sexual-orientation-gender/trans-identities).

INDEX

ABOUT THE AUTHOR

Corona Brezina is an author who has written over a dozen young adult books for Rosn Publishing. Several of her previous books have also focused on legal and social issues concerning teens, including *Personal Freedom and Civic Duty: Understanding Equal Rights* and *Helping a Friend Who Is Being Bullied*. She lives in Chicago.

PHOTO CREDITS

Cover, p. 14 Adam Hester/Blend Images/Getty Images; p. 5 Rex Features/AP Images; p. 8 Westend61/Getty Images; p. 12 HEX/Getty Images; p. 18 © Mark Wiener/Alamy Stock Photo; p. 20 © Lee Snider/Alamy Stock Photo; p. 23 © Blend Images/Alamy Stock Photo; p. 24 ZUMA Press, Inc./Alamy Stock Photo; pp. 27, 31, 34, 40, 43, 48 © AP Images; p. 29 Dan Burn-Forti/The Image Bank/Getty Images; p. 36 Leland Bobbe/The Image Bank/Getty Images; p. 38 SolStock/E+/Getty Images; p. 45 © Sean Drakes/Alamy Stock Photo; p. 46 © Queerstock, Inc./Alamy Stock Photo; p. 51 Asanka Brendon Ratnayake/Lonely Planet Images/Getty Images; cover and interior pages background graphic Shutterstock.com.

Designer: Nicole Russo; Editor: Elizabeth Schmermund;
Photo Researcher: Elizabeth Schmermund